My Heart's

Desire

The Exhortations Of A Loving Wife

My Heart's

Desire

The Exhortations Of A Loving Wife

SYLVIA M DALLAS

A publication of The Publisher's Notebook Ltd

My Heart's Desire – The Exhortations Of A Loving Wife

©2017, Sylvia M Dallas. All rights reserved

ISBN 978-976-96123-3-4

Cover Art: Dale Sewell

Published by: The Publisher's Notebook Ltd

Email: publisher@thepublishersnotebook.com

**THE PUBLISHER'S
NOTEBOOK LIMITED**
PUBLISHERS FOR THE CHRISTIAN GENRE

Dedication

To The Holy Spirit – Your love for me is strong, I feel Your embrace

To Rohan Anthony Dallas – His love for you is strong, My love for you is strong, feel our embrace

Scripture: John 6:37 "All that the Father gives me will come to me, and whoever comes to me I will never cast out."

Contents

Foreword

It is with great joy that I sit to pen my thoughts on this work "MY HEART'S DESIRE". In reading this work the first thing that came to mind is the cry of Abishag, Solomon first wife (whom he pet named "Shulamite" because of where she was born) "I AM LOVE SICK"

Song of Solomon 2:5 *"Sustain me with raisins; refresh me with apples, for I am sick with love."* (ESV)

It has been said that a woman speaks an average of twenty thousand words in a day (according to a study done by (Louann Brizendine; The University of California), but very few use these many words to actually express their love and encouragement to their husbands. This book therefore is a rarity, and at times left me wondering if there should not only be one copy published.

We have been invited into the deep and personal happenings in the writer's life and marriage, the struggles that sometimes goes on in her heart, when her will says "yes Lord" even if her emotions are saying "oh no, not this time." We see how words aptly spoken become a tool of grace rather than a weapon of emasculation. "THERE IS GREATNESS IN YOU" and "YOUR WORTH IS NOT BASED ON YOUR PAST" are some of the exhortations used.

Proverbs 25:11 *"A word fitly spoken is like apples of gold in a setting of silver"* *(ESV)*

Ephesians 4:29 *"Let no corrupting talk come out of your mouths, but only such as is good for building up, as fits the occasion, that it may give grace to those who hear"* *(ESV.)*

We are made to see that irrespective of the challenges and onlookers opinions, this wife can look at her husband and say it's not because you've earned it, in truth "YOU ARE WORTHY OF MY LOVE". It is no wonder then that this creates an atmosphere for miracles where a metaphor of persistent, stubborn, unwavering and enduring love can be found in a half-empty gas cylinder.

It my hope that:

• her husband will take to heart this expression of her love, *"... Husbands live with your wives (wife) in an understanding way, showing honor to the woman as the weaker vessel", since they (she) are heirs with you of the grace of life, so that your prayers may not be hindered.* **1Peter 3:7 (ESV)**

• Wives who read will take to pattern and give voice to their love for their husbands. *"A garden locked is my sister, my bride, a spring locked, a fountain sealed ..., Awake, O north wind, and come, O south wind! Blow upon my garden, let its spices flow. She Let my beloved come to his garden, and eat its choicest fruits".* **Song of Solomon 4:12-16 (ESV)**

- All others who read it will take as testimonial of the limitless depths that YHVH's (God's) love will go in order to reach fallen man. *"The LORD appeared to him from far away. I have loved you with an everlasting love; therefore I have continued my faithfulness to you"*. **Jeremiah 31:3 (ESV)**

Shalom
Rev. Wayne E. A. Palmer Dip.BS. B.Th.
Senior Apostle Jubilee Worship Centre

Preface

So here I am again, peacefully minding my own business. It is a birthday like no other. My husband, angry about where his life is heading, storms out of the house at 3:00 am. I grab him and pray for him before he leaves, asking the Lord to order his steps and praying that he will commit all his plans to the Lord. It takes everything out of me to do that because I am hurt by his actions.

Yesterday, my phone did a weird thing. It was not recognizing any of my SIM cards even though they are in the phone and when I checked, they worked in other phones. I am so used to receiving the first call on my birthday from my mother that at 51, I have not grown out of it. I miss the sound of her voice and her telling me the story of my birth which amuses me to this day. I can only communicate with Wi-Fi via WhatsApp or Facebook. I hate texting. I want to cry. Mostly, I just want my husband to come back, hug me and tell me he is sorry even though he knows I have already forgiven him.

I encourage myself in the Lord. I keep asking myself and commanding my soul – *"Why be downcast, O my soul? Hope thou in the Lord."* The Holy Spirit tells me as I am on the bus, *"You need to write this book."* The tears start to form, once again I have to expose my life to the public domain, but I do not hesitate – I just say yes. *"Sylvia, your experiences are not just for you. There are many hurting wives with Christian husbands who cannot understand what is happening to them. Your experience will resonate with them and bring healing."* There is a part of me that wants to say, "You know Holy Spirit, you have given me seven books to write about your Undying Love, must I put them down to write this?" But I know the answer already. I am not insensitive to God's timing.

At this time the church is calling men back into position, recognizing how chaotic it has become because men are not in their rightful place of leadership. Even in this week of prayer and fasting at my church, our focus is on the men. I recognize also that in walking in complete obedience to the promptings of the Holy

Spirit, I will experience this undying love as I die to my desires and seek God's desires to be my own.

*Why be downcast, O my soul.....*a whisper of the Word dries my tears.

I am sitting in a coffee house trying to figure out how I got here. I am trying to figure out how to write this book, which is basically love letters to my husband. Why am I writing it in a book?

- I want if for some reason our marriage does not survive, for him to remember how much he is loved, by Jesus and by me. It is not that I believe that we will break up, but he seems to have given up. It takes three to make a marriage work and thrive; husband, wife and Jesus.
- I want to encourage him in the Lord
- Some of my other married friends are in the same quandary that I am
- I want him to know that I am holding my position beside Jesus and that when He surrenders to His will, and finds his way back to Him,

he will find me there also. We will both greet him with open arms.

- Although Christianity has often been portrayed as a "woman thing", I want him to recognize that it takes balls to be a man of God. It is a "man" thing also. Jesus was no wimp. Each of us (man and woman) has our role to play in the Kingdom.

- Resonance – Oftentimes we think that we are alone in our experiences. But when others see that you not only survived but thrived because of your experience, hope grows in them.

Several times while in the coffee shop, I feel the tears forming. I recognize that this day can either be beautiful or disheartening, depending on what I allow. I command the atmosphere "Peace, be still" and calm returns to my space. No more heaviness in my heart, no more tears in my eyes.

I say, "Father I recognize that you have isolated me today for a reason, so let Your perfect will be done. I am not arguing with Your Holy Spirit, just tell me what to do and empower me." I am surrendered.

Sylvia M Dallas
June 9, 2016

My Favorite Days

The average person would think that my favorite day might have been my wedding day. They would be wrong. No, it was not the day I met you either. I have three favorite days where you are concerned. The first one occurred on June 17, 2011 when you accepted Jesus Christ as your Lord and Saviour. There was a rejoicing in heaven for you, but my heart was dancing. I was crying for the sheer joy of it.

Then you got baptized. I remember that morning. There were only two of you being baptized. It seemed as if the very seas and all the elements were raging. I remember praying as you went into the water, "Peace, be still."

My all-time favorite day was the day you received baptism of the Holy Spirit. We were attending our first prayer workshop together at church. Jacquie asked "Who wants to receive the baptism of the Holy Spirit?" You were one of three. The rest of us were on the right side of the church praying for Jamaica. The Holy Spirit prompted me to look to my left. There I saw you on the floor with your feet stretched out before you without shoes, praying in the language of the Holy Spirit, clapping your hands and weeping. I wished that I could have taken a picture of you then so that you could always remember the look of joy on your face, but the Holy Spirit directed me back to prayer. I asked you later about what I saw. I remember you saying "I had to untie my laces to put on back my shoes." That was so awesome to me because I knew that your shoes were of such that you could not take them off without pulling the laces, so I recognized the power that caused them to come off, with the laces still tied.

I looked forward to our prayer life together.

Rebellion In The House

I have long since repented before the Lord for this, not just in our marriage but for my previous marriage. The Lord rebuked me about rebellion. I asked Him, "How am I being rebellious?" He said that I should have been praying you into your position of leadership, not staging a coup. I asked Him for clarity. He showed me that in His order of things, you are the head of our home, and that I must be submitted to you. I really had a problem with the word "submitted." So many husbands and pastors have bludgeoned women with this scripture over the years. I was led by His Spirit to search out the meaning of the word. I realised that it means to respect you. I asked Him to show me how to respect you at all times. Instead of taking over, I searched out the Word for what should be your role in our marriage and I prayed those words over you.

Respecting you is not dependent on you respecting me. It means holding my correct position in the Word even if you are in the wrong. The fact is, you are the authority of our house. The things you say come to pass, the things you do have resounding repercussions.

In Deuteronomy, when Moses came out of the tabernacle, Joshua stayed in the Presence. This tells me that even if you, my authority leave the Presence of God, I must remain there.

For the many times I have rebelled against you in word, in deed and even in my heart, please forgive me.

Your Identity

With whom do you identify? I have seen you in moments of anger, revert to a thug-like behaviour. Yet, when you came in to covenant with God by accepting Jesus Christ, your identity changed. You are no longer your past. That was buried the day you accepted Him as your Lord and Saviour. You cannot know how to identify with Jesus if you do not read His Word. You cannot rely on what others tell you about the Bible. It is something you have to read for yourself.

I encourage you to search Him out through His Word. Find out what He loves to do, what His desires are, what His character entails and the things He hates. You are like Him for He says "be thou holy as I Am holy." God is not an unreasonable God. He will not tell us to do what we are unable to do. He will empower us with His Holy Spirit so that it is easy for us to be obedient.

The Day We said "I Do"

July 22, 2011. I remember that day well. As I reached the gate of my aunt's house where we were having the ceremony, I panicked. My palms were literally soaked and my knees felt weak. I turned to my sister and said 'Lainey I cannot do it." She never said anything – just waited. My thoughts were in chaos. I was thinking of my previously failed marriage. I wondered if we would last. I worried that you would abandon me. More *What-If* questions ran through my mind than an Excel spreadsheet.

In the midst of the chaos, a sudden calm enveloped me, and I felt peace. My palms dried and strength returned to my knees. I said to my sister – "Let's go in."

As George walked me up the aisle you did not wait by Pastor Redwood, you came to get me and there were tears in your eyes.

There Is Greatness In You

I remember once you expressed anger about my prayer life. Yet, you could not tell me of one instance where I neglected you because of this prayer life. I discerned that you were jealous of my relationship with God and said to you – "I cannot have your relationship with God for you. You have to cultivate that for yourself."

I looked at you and saw a man struggling with his past, the negative words spoken over his life, and his desire to better his life at any cost, in his own strength.

I hugged you, we wept together, we prayed together. In that beautiful moment, the Lord told me to tell you "There is greatness in you." I did and you looked at me in amazement.

This greatness cannot be achieved in your own strength. It has to be done through a life aligned with God's will.

My Favourite Person

Did you know that no matter how much you anger me, I am always glad to see you when you come through the door?

For me anger is temporary, too much of a burden to carry in my heart. I forgive you as soon as you hurt me with your words and/or indifference.

As we grew together, I have seen where you try to be more careful with your words and I appreciate that.

My love for you is a constant. It overrides any temporary feeling I might have. When you come home and I say "Yay – my favorite person is home!" I actually mean it.

Anything is not Anything

Do you know that I actually want and value your advice? When I ask your opinion on a matter and you answer "anything a anything" – that really does not give me much to work on or with. I ask for your advice because I value your input. Just because I do not respond in the manner you think I should, does not de-value your opinion in anyway.

I may not take all of your advice, but it does give me a guideline with which to work. Your perspective is unique and I respect it. I may not agree all the time but it does not make it any less valuable.

A More Excellent Way

There is always a better way to do things. I have seen you struggle when you do not have to. I am not saying that you will not have challenges in life. These are the things that make you stronger in faith, in resilience. But your reliance must not be on what you know that worked the last time. The God you serve is only predictable in His love for you, that it is constant and therefore can be relied upon.

Because God moved in a particular direction in your life yesterday, does not mean that is the path you should take today. Each day you need to seek Him and ask Him – "What must I do today? Where must I go? Give me divine appointments – an opportunity to talk about Your goodness. Order my steps today Lord."

One thing I am sure of, you hear the voice of the Holy Spirit clearly. He is the Spirit of Truth, the Teacher and the Comforter. You will hear His voice more clearly when you immerse yourself in His Word. He is ready and willing to teach you about the heart of God. With His Word hidden in your heart, you will not sin against Him. God sent us the Way, the Truth and the Life in the form of Jesus Christ His Son. **The Truth** is His Word. There is no lying in God. He is not the deceiver – the devil is. **The Life** is in Jesus Christ. Every action you take in your life is based on a decision to do or not to do. As a man of God, you should precede every decision with the question – "Is this what Jesus would do?" If you love Him, then you will want to do as He does, what He likes and you will hate to do the things that He hates. **The Way** is the direction that you follow when you open your heart to be totally submitted to Him. A heart of disobedience leads you in the wrong direction. Your way will never be as good as His Way, and He will never lead you to a path of destruction. Allow Him to show you the more excellent Way which is LOVE.

You **Are** Worthy Of My Love

I have heard time and time again from others how lucky you are to have me, as if you are undeserving of me loving you. I get tired of correcting these persons. I tell them we are blessed to have each other.

I am glad our relationship is a work in progress. As our pastors often say "we are working out the holiness in each other." Each challenge we face together and come through, undergird us and give us strength. Each one deals with our heart issues and perfects us in Christ.

We have grown in the Lord. I see where I have matured to the point where I do not give in to the rages that used to consume me. I have grown past the place of letting my emotions rule me and I have learned that our marriage is not all about me. O there has been quite a few times where you frustrated me to the point of asking God "Was this my decision or Yours?" Or, "did I consult You when I made this decision?" Yet each time the Holy Spirit reassures me that it is ok.

Despite the challenges and trials that we encounter, every day I thank God for you. I thank Him for the love we share. I thank Him for our marriage, your children – who have enriched my life in ways that are profound. I thank Him for our grandchildren whom He has given me to pour out my love upon. We are so blessed to have each other.

Your Worth Is **Not** Based On Your Past

I remember when it first became apparent to our community that we were in a relationship. I could not take a step without hearing about something that you "used to do". I countered every one of these accusations with "I know – he told me." Eventually, upon realising that I was not moved by your past, they stopped coming to me. ***I will never entertain gossip about you.***

The past has a way of echoing into our present and future – if we let it. The amount of negative comments I have heard pronounced over your life since I met you is astounding. I often ask my self – what if these people knew from where I was coming? They would be amazed.

If God was to use our past to judge us we would be in a sorry state. Yet He says He "remembers our transgressions no more". Shut down the echo of your past in your mind. Allow the Holy Spirit to free you from the cages that your mind has been locked into. When you do that, allow Him to lock that cage and throw away the key. The Word of God says that when you accepted Jesus Christ, the Spirit of Adoption came into you and by this Spirit you can say "Abba, Father." Your past does not exist in the mind of God. Do not allow the enemy to gain a foothold in your mind. Refuse to entertain the thoughts of inadequacy, of not being good enough, of failure. Embrace instead the Word of God which says BEFORE you were born He knew you. His plans for you are without harm, to prosper you, to give you a hope and a future. Embrace the fact that what you were unable to do in your past, you can now do all things through Christ who strengthens you.

Remember that God uses your tests to become testimonies and your messes to become messages. That is the only context in which your past has any relevance in your life.

The Half Empty Gas Cylinder

Do you remember the gas cylinder that we thought was empty? We exchanged it for a new one only to discover that it was the burner on the stove that was faulty. We had it returned and several weeks later we were still using the gas from that "empty" cylinder.

There have been frustrations aplenty in our marriage. Sometimes it might even feel like we have run out of love (the fuel of our marriage). Many persons that we know have run from one relationship to another as one would exchange gas cylinders thinking they have run out of love for that person. Yet if they had just eliminated what was at fault they would find that they would not have to exchange their "cylinders" because the "fuel" was still there.

I am happy that I have grown past the urge to "cut and run" whenever there was a problem. Our love has grown stronger to the point where one day when I felt that

I had run out of love, I asked God to "love you through me." He refilled and refuelled me and no exchange was necessary.

The Pittance vs The Abundance

There was a woman who came to Jesus asking for healing for her daughter. She was a Syro-Phoenician woman, that is, not a Jew. Jesus answered and said to her that He had come for the House of Israel and that it was not fitting for Him to take the bread meant for the Children of Israel and feed it to the dogs. Yet she pressed in and told Him that even the dogs get crumbs from the table. He rewarded her faith.

Firstly, this woman decided that for what she was after, she could not afford to take offense at what He said.

Secondly, she was willing to settle for the crumbs – to take whatever she could get to achieve her purpose – healing for her daughter. She decided that crumbs from Jesus' table were far greater than anything else she could have received.

Thirdly, her faith was rewarded.

You might be wondering what you have in common with this woman.

I have seen you miss church to pursue fishing, hunting, cooking. Yet each time, I see you come back with little or nothing and frustrated. Example, you might leave for fishing because the weather seems good (on the very night you are to go to Dominion Fire – bible study) – yet when you get to the seaside, the weather is so bad that you cannot go out. Usually I hear a Word from God that I know would have connected with your spirit. The enemy had just tricked you and caused you to miss something vital for the enrichment of your soul.

Perhaps your reasoning is that is better for you to earn a small amount and miss church than earn nothing.

The crumbs of the world cannot compare to the crumbs from God's table.

Yet, He does not want you to eat crumbs. He is not interested in giving you pittance – He wants you to feast at the table. He desires to enrich and prosper you in all areas of life. He wants to pour in the oil of healing and the wine of gladness. He knows all that you need beforehand and has prepared it for you. All you have to do is believe and ask. His Word says it is His good pleasure to give you the Kingdom.

Yet, if you are willing, like this woman, to only take the crumbs from **His** table, your faith will be rewarded.

Whom My Soul Lovest

As you know, I listen to the Song of Songs a lot. I have often thought Chapter 3 verse 1:

"by night on my bed, I sought Him whom my soul lovest"

I ponder what it means in terms of my relationship with Jesus and for our marriage. These verses incite a passion in me to worship before God and experience a deeper intimacy with Him.

I find also that the more deeply intimate I get with Him, is the greater my desire for you. This means, I yearn for you in every way; in a spiritual and physical sense. It grows into a longing and a thirst that only you can quench.

Although your spirit man seems far from me, almost unreachable – I remember that we took a vow and became *one flesh*. I pray that the Lord will spring up a well within you. A deep hunger and thirst for His Presence.

I pray even as Jeremiah declared that the Word of God was shut up in his bones like fire, so will the desire for His Living Flame consume you.

You are whom my soul loves – for we are one flesh.

Your Pearls of Wisdom

I remember the day we were coming from one of our hikes in the bush. I was so exhausted, I could barely put one foot in front of the other. We were in a clearing among some trees and I just wanted to lie down.

As you saw me putting down my gear, you stopped me and asked me to walk a few more steps to the edge of the clearing. When we reached, you showed me our community just about a half mile away. I had thought the distance was much further.

You said to me, "See, there is home. *The hardest part of any journey is closest to home"*

Another time while we were hiking, we were on top of a cliff overlooking a forest that we would be moving through. You said to me, *"You need to see the overall picture. We are starting here (you indicated our starting point) and we are going to end up there (the destination). As we move through the forest it will not be easy, there will be a lot of bending and twisting, but we will be coming out."*

I remember that hike as if it was yesterday. The bending under bushes, climbing over tree trunks bigger than me (so it seemed), rocky terrain, and rock faces to climb (thankfully not too long) was agonizing to my untrained body. Each time I remembered the big picture and your words *"..but we will be coming out."* I was unafraid because I knew that all I had to do was to keep you in sight, and if I could not see you, I could call and you would come. It was comforting knowing you were never too far from me.

Sometimes in our marriage we have faced these situations. The troubling times of the past were not easy and I am sure that the future will have its challenges. I have seen the big picture though. I have seen the hand of God in our marriage. If we just keep Him in sight, or call on Him if we lose sight of Him we will be at peace in any situation.

I Cannot Know If You Do Not Tell Me

There have been times when you have said to me that I have no idea what you can do. Sometimes you say that I do not know what skills you have. My answer: Show me, tell me.

I cannot know your desires if you do not tell me. I cannot know your plans if you do not tell me.

Communication is vital to any relationship. Without it each person feels like they are in a vacuum, unable to understand the void around them.

Talk to me. I never get tired of listening to you. Most of the things that lift me out of the doldrums are things that you have said to make me laugh. But that is not all I want. I want to know what it is that you dream about achieving, how you plan to achieve it and how I can fulfill my role as your help meet to support your desires.

If you cannot remember how much I admire you, let me remind you:

- I think you are a genius
- I love your dry sense of humour
- I love your ambition
- I love your sense of focus
- I believe that there is nothing that is impossible for you to achieve
- I love the fact that you are such a powerful man of prayer, because I have seen that when you pray things happen really quickly. It's as if God is just waiting to hear a prayer from you to put it into action
- I appreciate everything that you do to make my life comfortable
- I think you are the most Alpha of males
- You are THE REAL BIG MAN

There are other thoughts that I have about you but I'll just whisper those to you.

About The Author

Sylvia M Dallas, born June 9, 1965 accepted Jesus Christ as her Lord and Saviour at the age of 10 years. It was at that time that she discovered her gift for writing. In 2000 she published her first book under the pseudonym Gina Rey Forest and several books later on. In 2007 she declared unto God, "I will not perform on stage again, or write another poem unless it glorifies You". She was immediately tested. She received several offers to perform her previous style of sensuous poetry with pay. She turned them all down. In 2011, she recommitted her life to God, promising to be obedient to His Word and the promptings of His Holy Spirit. This is her fourth book since recommitting to Christ. She has been married to Rohan Dallas since 2011.